POCKET GUIDE TO MEETING NEW PEOPLE

Pocket Guide To Meeting New People

How To Turn Complete Strangers Into Friends

ANDY LEE GRAHAM

HoboTraveler.com EverydayHobo.com

INTRODUCTION

How To Meet New People: How To Turn Complete Strangers Into Friends

> *"One of the joys of travel is visiting new towns and meeting new people."*
> - Genghis Khan

A list of ways strangers decide to start talking with you; this is a valuable skill for photographers, lovers, friends, and businesses. I estimate the average person meets 5-15 new people per day, this book gives ideas on how to seize then unclaimed opportunities. How to turn a casual glance, or eye contact into a conversation with complete strangers.

While searching on Google for ways to meet people, few gave the way, the strategies, instead they listed out clever lines, as if I was trying to seduce a woman with clever lines. This book is about first principles, the starting point, and how to get people willing to talk with you.

Please read the book, *"How to Win Friends and Influence People,"* a self-help book written by Dale Carnegie in 1936. I wish it was required reading in schools. Dale's book profoundly outlines the do's and don'ts of how to win friends and keep them as friends. After you meet a person, after you open a conversation, this book is genius, the best of the best.

"How To Meet New People" is the missing chapter in the book by Dale Carnegie. After a conversation is opened, we can then win friends, and influence people, but first, we can learn, *"How to Open Conversations.",*

This is the sequence of a conversation:

1. **We open conversations**
2. We win friends.
3. And influence people.

The normal person has 5-20 opportunities per day to talk.

I have been a non-stop world traveler now for 25-plus years. I do not have a home, I have lived in 114 countries; occasionally I stop in the USA to say hello to family and friends. I do not own a house or a car, I live as a traveler.

I write a Blog and create YouTube videos explaining how to be a world traveler. First things first, one must create an endless stream of money, best to have 1000 to 2000 dollars per month. Many retired people become travelers when they start receiving Social Security, or a pension. There is a new group called "Digital Nomads," who work remotely, maybe their employer is in the USA, and there is no reason for them to come to the office. People who have monthly income can be world travelers.

After a lot of soul-searching, I asked myself,
"Andy, what are you doing differently, why do you enjoy traveling endlessly?"

In June of 2023, I watched a video summary of the book, "The Unfair Advantage," by Ash Ali and Hasan Kubba. Then in an ironic twist of fate, the next day, I spoke with Rich Gedney, one of the members of EverydayHobo.com, and he said,

"You are good at capturing street photography."

Rich astutely pointed out one of my natural skills, something I take for granted.

I asked myself, "Andy, what is your unfair advantage?"

Why can you travel endlessly?

The answer is, I don't get lonely, I can open a conversation with 5-20 people daily, and I am always surrounded by new friends. This unfair advantage also helps me to take street photos, and make youtube videos. - Thank you, Rich Gedney.

Then using the guidance of Dale Carnegie, I win them as friends, keep them as friends, and our friendships grow. I have friends in over 100 countries. If we can open a conversation, then we are never alone.

This book is to share an evolving, growing list of ways to give you an unfair advantage when opening a conversation. I hope you used Dale Carnegie's book to win friends, and influence people.

The more people we meet, the more opportunities.

Thank you, Andy Lee Graham
CEO HoboTraveler Inc.
EverydayHobo.com Social Network

This book is dedicated to "Popcorn."

Me sitting around eating popcorn, and sharing with new friends was the motivation for this book. I have met dozens of people by sharing my popcorn in public.
Thank you, Andy Lee Graham

YOUR PERSONAL NOTES

Please write on this page new ways to meet complete strangers.

Copyright © 2023 by Andy Lee Graham

All rights reserved. No part of this book may be reproduced in any manner whatsoever without written permission except in the case of brief quotations embodied in critical articles and reviews.

First Printing, 2023

CONTENTS

Introduction — iv
Dedication — ix
Your Personal Notes — xi
I Write For Fun — xvii

1. Introduced By Friends — 1
2. Permission Granted Social Events — 3
3. A Person Starts Talking To You — 6
4. When We Say Thank You — 8
5. Do You Want To Dance — 10

XIV - CONTENTS

6	Cats And Dogs	11
7	Children	13
8	Just Start Talking - Fishing	14
9	Head On A Swivel. Smile And Eye Contact	15
10	Daily Regular At Store, Coffee, Etc.	17
11	Sharing Anything	19
12	Introduce Yourself	20
13	Questions Strangers Want To Answer	22
14	Wave After Eye Contact	24

CONTENTS - XV

15	Say Hello In Foreign Language	26
16	Help Someone	28
17	Name Tags	30
18	Go To A Group Of People Talking	32
19	Read Words On Shirt	34
20	Write a Letter or Email	36
21	Sit Close To People	38
22	Give A Gift	39
23	Peacocking	40
24	Give A Business Card	42

XVI - CONTENTS

| 25 | Popcorn | 44 |

Suggest Ways To Meet People 47

I WRITE FOR FUN

How to weigh the success of this book?

If you meet one new friend.

This book was written for people who want to enjoy life, I write for fun. There are two types of readers, the ones that look for what is right with life, and all the others.
Life is good.
 - Andy Lee Graham

| 1 |

Introduced By Friends

Introduced By Friends

This is the number one way to open a conversation.

Explained:

Friends are happy to introduce you to people they know, the more friends you have the more introductions.

Optimization:

1. When you see a friend talking to a person you

wish to meet, go over and join them.
2. Learn to remember the names of people.
3. There are friends who have more friends, make a note of the people who have introduced you to friends.

| 2 |

Permission Granted Social Events

Permission Granted Social Events

For example, at church, Rotary Club, and Cocktail parties permission is granted by attendance to go over and talk with a person you do not know.

Explained:

People are granted permission in advance so that when they attend social events, strangers will approach them and talk.

Optimization: List of examples.

- Bars
- Public Transport
- Volunteer Work
- Book Club Meetings
- Local Meetups
- Dog Parks
- Gym
- Local Museum
- Bus Tour
- Music Club
- Airport
- Family Functions
- Hiking
- Yoga Class
- Local Running Races
- Weekend Classes
- Your Local Neighborhood
- Cultural Event
- Debate Club
- Community Centers
- On a Trip
- Coffee Shop
- Charity Work
- Part-Time Job
- At Your Workplace

- Stadiums
- Outside a Store
- Bookstore
- Informal Gatherings
- Anonymous Meetings
- Study Circles
- Wedding
- Protests
- Sports Team
- Dance Class
- Professional Networking Groups
- Religious Groups or Cultural Clubs
- Facebook Groups & Events
- Music & Art Festivals
- Friendship Apps
- Chat Rooms and Forums
- Meetup.com
- Open House
- Online Courses
- Video Games and Mobile Games

| 3 |

A Person Starts Talking To You

A Person Starts Talking To You

When a person starts talking to you, it's an opportunity.

Explained:

There are always a few people who start talking to smiling people, it's easy to open a conversation.

Optimization:

1. Repeat to yourself, I have permission to talk to

strangers.

2. Look at the person bravely.

| 4 |

When We Say Thank You

When We Say Thank You

To open a conversation, we seize and expand on conversations.

Explained:

There are dozens of times a person can say thank you during a day. Saying thank you is an acceptable conversation, there is no stigma, and there is no offense taken. The conversation is open with thank you, and one can keep the conversation open, it's a powerful time, full of appreciation, and care.

Optimization:

1. Look people in the eyes.
2. Expand the thank you. For example, we can say Thank you, when are you going to sell these flowers again?
3. Any response to thank you is a benefit, when a person says you are welcome, that stops. However, many people who want to talk will add more words, when more than welcome is said, this is our opportunity to open longer conversations.

| 5 |

Do You Want To Dance

Do You Want To Dance
This is a sub-category of "Permission Granted Social Events," but includes the possibility of love.

Explained:
Asking a person to dance is the courtship of a person for a lover, and love makes the world go round.

Optimization:
1. Maybe take classes in dancing.
2. Keep the drinking of alcohol to a minimum.

| 6 |

Cats And Dogs

Cats And Dogs

Instantly, two people have something in common, Cats, and Dogs, pets are super conversation openers.

Explained:

People love their cats and dogs. I believe because our pets can be touched by other people with little problem, this conversation open is better than children.

Optimization:

1. Walk in a manner to show your cats and dogs.

2. Stop to allow bystanders to come to praise your pets.

3. It is possible that pet clothing can increase the odds of opening a conversation.

| 7 |

Children

Children

The majority of people have children, or dream of having children.

Explained:

In my opinion, if we were more like children, there would be no need for this book. Children are happy, and playful and endear themselves with ease.

Optimization:

1. This could be controversial, so I will not enter my thoughts.

| 8 |

Just Start Talking - Fishing

Just Start Talking - Fishing
My friend Rich Gedney recommended this.

Explained:
This is how people who have never met a person who is not their friend engages with people, they are in conversations with everyone around them.

Optimization:
1. Do not demand answers, or expect answers.
2. You are fishing for anyone that replies.

| 9 |

Head On A Swivel. Smile And Eye Contact

Head On A Swivel. Smile And Eye Contact
To be safe in this world, best to have your head on a swivel.

Explained:
Rotate your head from left to right, from right to left, inspecting everything along your path. If you smile, and make eye contact, you will attract a few people's attention, and they will start talking.

Optimization:

1. Do not walk with a mission to your destination and do not be in any hurry to arrive.
2. Focus on the people who return a smile, and say hello.
3. If you walk the same paths, after a few days you have permission to talk.

| 10 |

Daily Regular At Store, Coffee, Etc.

Daily Regular At Store, Coffee, Etc.

After a face becomes familiar, we have permission to talk.

Explained:

We can go to the same convenience shop, same coffee shop, and even the same gas station daily. To be a regular means you also get permission to talk.

Optimization:

1. Say hello daily, greet, smile, and use people's names.
2. When a person says more than hello back, this is an opportunity.

| 11 |

Sharing Anything

Sharing Anything

Permission is granted to open a conversation.

Explained:

You can be sharing the kitchen in Hostel. You can be sharing seats on the plane. You can be sharing the sidewalk, anywhere you must agree to be with another person, there is the inferred right to talk.

Optimization:

1. Choose where you sit.
2. There is no reason to talk with unhappy, gloomy people.

| 12 |

Introduce Yourself

Introduce Yourself

This is blunt but highly effective.

Explained:

Say excuse me, then introduce yourself, shake hands if possible, the start on one the 100's of topics of people.

Optimization:

1. Works best if you are very handsome, or beautiful
2. Do not apologize.

3. Have a reason why you introduced yourself.
4. Do not have an agenda, or be deceptive.

| 13 |

Questions Strangers Want To Answer

Questions Strangers Want To Answer

There are questions that illicit empathy, and sympathy.

Explained:

There are special questions, that everyone in a group wants to answer, for example, "Where is the restroom?" People seldom will refuse to answer.

Optimization:

Is it raining outside?

Where is the restroom?
Is it safe to walk down that street?
What language are you speaking?
Which country?
Do you live in this city?
Where are the police?
Where is the bus stop?
Do I know you?
I saw you yesterday at...

Please help us expand on this list.

Write Andy Lee Graham hoboontheroad@yahoo.com

| 14 |

Wave After Eye Contact

Wave After Eye Contact

There are people who appreciate polite waves of the hand.

Explained:

Say for example you are sitting in the park, and a person looks over at you; we can seize the opportunity and give a polite wave. Wait, maybe they will come over and talk.

Optimization:

1. Be open to them coming over to talk with you.
2. Best to not go towards them.

POCKET GUIDE TO MEETING NEW PEOPLE - 25

| 15 |

Say Hello In Foreign Language

Say Hello In Foreign Language

Most people consider it nice when a foreigner says hello.

Explained:

Jack, a Canadian I met in Acapulco, Mexico, used to advise me, "Andy, stop saying hello in Spanish if you want to talk to people." Then followed up by saying, "The locals want to know you are from the USA."

This works the same in the USA, I can say "Bon Jour" to a person, and this creates a curious conversation.

Optimization:
1. Say this to a group, and see whose eyes are awakened.
2. Spanish is not the best language for the USA, try European languages.

| 16 |

Help Someone

Help Someone

There is nothing more human than helping someone, we are social animals.

Explained:

There are dozens of opportunities to be helpful during the day if we leave the house.

Optimization:

1. Look in the eyes of people, and you can see their need for help.
2. Giving money is not help that creates friendship.

POCKET GUIDE TO MEETING NEW PEOPLE

| 17 |

Name Tags

Name Tags
Name tags are helpful in business, they also create friendships.

Explained:
There are name tags everywhere, when you see one, read the name out loud, people like to hear their names.

Optimization:
1. Read the book by Dale Carnegie, his explanations of names are genius.

2. The name tag is there to be used, do not feel guilty reading a name out loud.

| 18 |

Go To A Group Of People Talking

Go To A Group Of People Talking

Simple, where there are people talking, we meet people.

Explained:

There are groups of people talking in many places. For example, the McDonald's restaurant in Angola, Indiana has a daily breakfast group. If I go over and sit next to them, soon I will be included in the conversation, and meet people.

POCKET GUIDE TO MEETING NEW PEOPLE - 33

Optimization:

1. Be extremely polite when meeting groups, Maybe best to wait until they ask your name, etc.

2. Write these locations where you encountered groups on the diary page at the front of this book.

| 19 |

Read Words On Shirt

Read Words On Shirt

10-25 percent of people are wearing shirts with words.

Explained:

People wear shirts with words on them to read, admire, and enjoy. In foreign countries they often do not understand the words, a great way to meet people is to translate the words on their shirts.

Optimization:

1. Read the words out loud for the room to hear.

2. Do not assume they understand the words on the shirt.

| 20 |

Write a Letter or Email

Write a Letter or Email
I write many well-known people's emails, introducing myself, and asking questions.

Explained:
When an email is posted, for example on YouTube channels, we can write them. How to get people to reply is art.

Optimization:
1. Fan mail will seldom get replies.
2. Empathize with the person, and write an enigmatic question that stimulates them to think.

3. Remember they are people, and have feelings, and curiosity.

| 21 |

Sit Close To People

Sit Close To People

This will double the number of people you meet in life.

Explained:

When I walk into any room on the planet, I look at the faces, then sit down close to the people I would like to meet. I am always open to having a good talk.

Optimization:

1. Eye contact, or a smile is permission to talk.
2. All people want to talk if they feel safe.

| 22 |

Give A Gift

Give A Gift

Generosity is rewarded.

Explained:

It may seem old-fashioned to you, but girls still like a box of chocolates. The person next to you appreciates when you buy him, or her a beer.

Optimization:

1. Do not have an agenda, do not expect anything more than friendship.
2. Gifts work exceptionally well when a person forgot to bring money.

| 23 |

Peacocking

Peacocking
There appears to be a peacock competition on the planet.

Explained:
Peacocking is when a person uses ostentatious clothing and behavior to attract attention, with the intention to become more memorable and interesting. People will come up and ask you about your clothing, or behavior.

Optimization:

POCKET GUIDE TO MEETING NEW PEOPLE - 41

1. Ask yourself, why do I dress the way I do? Why do I have one too many tattoos?

| 24 |

Give A Business Card

Give A Business Card
This is the number one way to be remembered.

Explained:
When I want to meet a person, especially a woman, I hand them my business card, and many start to text message. A business card says you are a person to be remembered.

Optimization:
1. Leave one anytime you are near a person of interest.

2. This empowers the person you want to meet, they can make the decision to become your friend.

| 25 |

Popcorn

Popcorn

I have met many girls with popcorn, it's the reason I wrote this book.

Explained:

This was explained in Chapter 11 on sharing. When we share our popcorn, we demonstrate we are a generous and friendly person.

The photo on the back of the book was taken in Togo, West Africa, they sell this popcorn in this manner. I can also buy 2-3, and make them small gifts.

Optimization:

1. The smaller the gift, the smaller the share, the better, best to not make a person feel obligated to be nice.

This book is dedicated to "Popcorn."

I thank you, life is good.
Andy Lee Graham

SUGGEST WAYS TO MEET PEOPLE

Send suggestions for ways to meet friends to: Andy Lee Graham, at hoboontheroad@yahoo.com, Include your full name, city, and country and I will include you in Volume II of this book.

Thank you, your new friend, Andy Lee Graham

www.ingramcontent.com/pod-product-compliance
Lightning Source LLC
Chambersburg PA
CBHW050446010526
44118CB00013B/1711